Therapeutic:
Soul Searching Poetry

Limited Edition

BLACK AUSAR

Published and Edited by Jason L. Shankle

AUTHOR

Black Ausar has been writing poetry since the age of 10. His pen served as a way to comfort himself during the dark moments in childhood and adolescences which transcended into philosophical poetry entries. As a creative writer it became his therapeutic medicine to express emotions he couldn't voice. The layout of his compilations of poems brings you along an unforgettable warrior walk through the streets, dreams and love... The heart of who he is now and evolution of himself lives in every word. He currently resides in Denver, Colorado.

Social Media Outlets:
Facebook, Instagram, Tik Tok & YouTube Channel:
@Book.King.Publishing

Books available on website:
www.bkingpublishing.com

Dedicated

To Jason Shankle, Jr. and my daughter Jael Shankle.

TABLE OF CONTENT

~*SPIRITUAL*~

My World

Ever since I was born,

I was doomed from the start,

But I have graces of God tattooed on my heart,

Sayings behind my mouth with art on my brain,

Trying to get it right before I go insane,

Even when it's sunny outside it feels like rain,

A beautiful sculptured picture frozen up in a frame,

I only get one life so I'm to blame,

Wishing to go back in the past and change some thing's,

No one's perfect in this world so I've got to adjust,

Living in this world with others is hard enough,

Got my life that's always a plus,

Some days I feel like I'm living just cause,

I know I'm here for a reason because He puts in my dreams,

And I can see me being freed from these,

Earthly sins, demons, and thieves,

If you don't believe in God,

These words should be making you think,

Why every night I pray to the Lord my soul to keep.

Keep Me

Making it is doing things you don't want to do,

In order to do what you want to do,

With few tools to help you,

Rules are met to be broken so why follow them?

People that aren't in your corner why call them?

Already knew how it was so why fault them?

Or kin when you're still breathing and not bleeding,

People still dying for dumb reasons,

Talking about what they had but now their leaving,

All you can say is,

I hope they believed in a Higher God,

All the times it could have been me,

He redeemed and continued to keep me,

Some nights I pray for God not to leave me,

But when I wake in the morning,

It is a brand-new way instead of past bad days,

To see moments ready for me,

I ask for God to keep me,

In the right state of mind,

Protect when I'm out on any grind,

There's no money without time,

And being hungry is overdue,

Wondering how it is to go crazy or mad,

Wanting stuff the devil doesn't want you to have,

Happiness feels like a flash but never be sad,

Being kept is how I'm going to last.

Eternal War

What goes around comes around,

Like a used round doing 360's on the ground,

In the mind trying to find-found,

Only remember dark nights on greyhounds,

If freedom's a lie,

Truth has a guilty conscience,

Passionate dreams lying in a bed of coals,

Heaven is high while Hell's lower,

Fine art between right and wrong,

Draw it over,

This world of skin needs poetic tattooists,

Writing images of ink in blood,

Step back then fall in Love,

Married to peace,

Hate an ugly divorce,

To have joy there must be war,

Not with the earth but the inner self,

Praying for help while killing "the self",

Pain is a symptom of weakness dying,

Lock and loaded prepared for battle,

Aiming at change in this land of epiphanies.

Somebody's Praying for Me

I remember numerous nights,

When it seemed like my life was derailed,

Drinking countless times,

Reminiscing on my timeline,

Alone in the room,

Thinking about thinking,

I'm still standing and only bruised,

More knowledge than you think outside the school,

Number one rule is respect,

Pray every night with purpose,

For the visions to paint pictures,

Walking in my dreams of new things,

Although nothing is free,

Without you there's no me,

I've seen many bad things,

That's how I know someone is praying for me.

Finally, Free

My mind keeps me in prison at times,

Shall I open this door for air or stay?

While I still have this joy in heart and soul,

Thus, free from vicious thieves with faulty schemes,

To be cuffed furthermore waiting for release hurts,

My eyes are guides through dark grim paths,

Remember me if you do lose your "true-self",

Be sure to breathe every breath of life,

My first, last to present including future,

The loss of time is forever long lost,

Searching for the key,

This cell is full of prayers in thoughts that dream,

From life until death,

My strive is true freedom,

Unlock these chambers finally,

I'm free.

Reflections of Truth

Mountaintops of achievement are high as the stars,

Images from afar show this art,

Despite low dark valleys,

This impact of strife changes views,

Weather is temporary sometimes even irrelevant,

The weight of waiting is heavy enough,

With mirrors serving as reminders,

Visionary pride everything's on the line,

If the truth is in the eye of the beholder,

Imagine what is in the mind?

Be careful when believing in what you see,

It could be vanity.

Soldier

Soldier of God,

Against all odds,

Look at the world and pause,

This it?

Or is it more than this?

Is it about the knowledge of wisdom?

Would I ask the same question minus faults?

Adversaries opposing victory,

For subconscious reasons,

With no if's, ands, buts or we,

My tongue is sharpened to cut through distortion,

Trying to survive daily arrows,

In this arena of the Universe.

Forgotten

Body worn and torn even famine,

I had energy when I laid down,

What is so different about today?

My alarm goes off on schedule,

But I don't feel the same way,

Without thinking all I could do was rest,

Each minute is a patient interview,

Physically the flesh says "no",

My mind says "yes",

While waiting for this challenge to finish,

Curiosity struck my senses like caffeine highs,

I reply "God",

Because of my routine I have forgotten me,

And just as difficult to explain,

The Most High is never late,

Persistently diligent in waking me up,

Even when I forget.

L.I.P.

Live In Peace,

Rest when sleep,

Rude people speak,

Judge on appearance,

Until you talk,

Rather have spirituality,

Than prejudice flaws,

Easy to see,

Small minds with big egos,

Will never fly high as eagles,

Grudges meet greed,

Only one thing,

It can cost you everything,

Before-thought,

At the end of this journal,

To my journey on Earth,

Heavens a paradise,

Where all the legends reside,

I know many happy people up there,

So, choose autonomy and prepare for now,

Why not smile?

Enemies destroy themselves,

God truly does help,

If you're genuine in effort,

To get past invisible blocks,

That tripped giants,

Enjoy life when it's simple,

Money corrupts souls,

Main reason why the little I have is abundant,

Every day is a boon.

<u>Rite</u>

If you write it in pencil,

It can be edited,

If you write it in pen,

It can't be erased,

If you write it in stone,

It must be destroyed,

If you write it in your heart,

It will be kept.

Listen

I don't know where the Most High is leading me,

Not being able to get a job makes me feel left out from the world,

But the purpose of having a job is to provide,

It is the root of most evil so what am I sighing for?

And the idols of many who are lost,

Maybe it's the Most High telling me,

Our relationship isn't good enough?

I am preparing to give you,

I feel like you left me,

I pray every night with no energy,

Trying to fix my own heart not knowing,

But know you are in the back of my mind,

When you should be in the front,

Why would you leave me?

When I cry these invisible tears while my heart bleeds,

It seems like my hope is gone…,

Never did I think writing poetry would be my remedy,

Yahweh, I know I am your child,

I do believe in you when we speak,

So, as I see others happy I am not jealous,

It's only confusion to me,

No one feels my pain,

How would I know?

Help me, I can't seem to connect or realize you are saving me,

In my heart I don't want to give up but my flesh is fighting,

The only thing that counts is my soul,

I can't hear your voice anymore,

Why give me this doubt?

The flame you have instilled is flickering,

I don't know what to do,

Listen, I am finally listening...

Educated Gangster

What an adrenaline rush I get from knowledge,

Collecting books like bullets for my last clip,

My mentality is militant,

Without a threat used but conveyed with respect,

Bold professionalism that would make Obama say,

Well done!

The canvas has changed,

These street corner light posts,

Transcended into desks lamp glares,

Writing papers as if I am articulating faith in ink,

To the parole board to be freed,

Heat only increases per degree,

Associate degree is the first temperature gauge,

Because your association is your representation,

Bachelors signifies the separation from others,

We know the crab in the bucket saying,

Just boil the water and hope for lobster,

Will you choose passion or will love choose you?

If your love is in money,

There is more to be learnt and discerned,

This plan is outlined like the Metu Neter volumes,

To adapt to conditions for victory,

Abiding by these 48 Laws of Power,

Hustlers lose when they die,

While words on documents represent physical form,

Master degree is the next level,

When you have children to feed,

One will master difficult things,

It is lucid to see that,

This is a game you play by default,

No choice and all involuntary admission,

History haunts everything,

Even when it isn't the truth,

Indefinitely we call it the past,

Tragedy may be expunged but always tracked,

That same compassion combined with self-actualization,

Transferring from finger on the trigger,

To thumb turning pages in a textbook,

Education is the deadliest tool,

Enlightenment seem further than drugs,

So, I went hard,

Doctorate of Philosophy,

Principle and obligation disperse intellect,

Courtrooms for classrooms,

And wise doctrines instead of plea bargains,

Professors are generals,

Strategize like W.E.B. DuBois,

It takes just as much consciousness to sell dope,

How do you kill a never-ending river?

A person who knows everything knows nothing,

Product of their environment,

Creating this shape of a chessboard,

Adversaries are thirsty for war,

You can't say gangsters are not educators,

Nor can educators not be gangsters?

In their own light,

Making students into soldiers,

For this world warfare,

Do they both not influence the masses?

Label us erudites.

Like Minds

Malcolm X's, creed by any means necessary,

Dr. King's humility and ability to dream,

Fred Hamptons preparation before a speech,

Tupac's tenacity with a Biggie size ego,

Lethal ether Illmatic as Nas,

Jay-Z's blueprint for the hustle,

Winning wordsmith taking the Big L,

Influential with a Lil' Wayne in the veins,

Confident as "Through the Wire" Kanye,

Tell a hood story like Scarface,

Z-RO tolerance if there's no payoff,

Persevering Earth, Wind and Fire,

Navigating this Frankie Beverly and Maze,

Pulling from old memories for Young Jeezy motivation,

Views of inspiration create this expression,

Like minds.

Pen and Pad

The blood from this pen reflects my heart,
Paper is the canvas made of skin,
Lies will die and the truth will never part.

Life is a chessonopoly game in the midst of art,
Weathering the storm and winds:
The blood from this pen reflects my heart.

This odyssey has been detailed and far,
Re-birth is where it begins:
Lies will die and the truth will never part.

Despite foolish decisions one must be smart,
There is no such thing as a secret:
The blood from this pen reflects my heart.

Believing in something is a start,
This process of trend happens over again:
Lies will die and the truth will never part.

Down the line a period separates pivotal parts,
The pulse of my identity flows through this pad:
The blood from this pen reflects my heart.

Lies will die and the truth will never part.

Liberated by Haters

Never confuse authenticity with empty communication,

Losers always lose while endurance wins victories,

Spirituality comes from the inside,

Tolerated pains in life is the enemies invite,

The envious uplift one's name behind closed doors,

Jealous fools operate in a paradox,

We know how the saying goes "they flock",

An indicator of character,

The Higher One rises the more others want you to die,

Never crossing the finish line,

A stupid question would be "why?"

It's evident,

Hate is blind.

Dreams

I sleep in army fatigue because of wars in my dreams,

It seems as if the devil thinks he can take things,

Without it being a fight,

Countdown during the day that never ends at night,

That's probably why fight and night go together so right,

Think about it?

If everything were right would there be a fight?

Or would the fight be living right?

And if so would there still be love songs?

Inquiries being answered like how come?

Never ask a question you don't desire an answer to,

The result may be silence,

It may be loud,

By yourself in a room,

Or alone in a crowd,

Looking to press forward despite flaws,

Every intention not to fall or fail,

But to excel far from hell and jail,

Changing the influence of my ways,

When finally done problems steady come,

Rejuvenating energy to get victory I must dream.

Road Ahead

To get to the top,

You must come from the bottom,

Why have a problem if you have the solution?

Never understood people who tell lies with every word,

If you can't accommodate in a relationship,

There is nothing to get,

Always stay mild in weather,

When it rains it pours,

Like hot bullets in Cold War,

Truth came from the core,

Taking the hinges off the door for entrance,

Simply because this world is a whirlwind,

Irony is easy,

Common clichés like knowledge is gold,

Enemies will sweep over your feet,

Ways are direction to destinations,

Leading avenues and hidden back streets,

This road ahead only appears further.

Expression

Don't get so uptight when you read this,

Saying is this about me?

Could this be who the author is?

So, you know me?

I know you?

No one knows anybody,

Critics feel entitled like air in the atmosphere,

My mind wouldn't be strong if I believed you?

Judging judgment,

Now I may offend,

Indirect methods are for cowards,

Subliminal for the unconscious,

Choose positivity over slothfulness,

And smile every once in a while,

Detach your emotions to look at this portrait of art,

It's just expression….

Declare War

Woke up felt strange in the air,

Usually its change like past days fear,

Cold heartedness is mental,

Most people show you the mask before their face,

Seven deadly sins have a lot in common,

Living in a dimension of perception,

Fuels dry hate aspiration,

Serious as a brain operation,

"Love money" makes a full sentence,

Those who navigate scrutiny,

If I don't have love,

I can't prevail,

Beyond trenches of tragedy,

Pure lenses stare in my world-view,

Focus on influence over change,

Because it spreads quicker,

I declare war on me,

To equate a better, we.

My Edit

Past then greater than better,

Whether weather effects my environment,

Your longitude and latitude determine attitude,

Faster than your rational thought,

Deep in good music,

The sole of my soul on earth,

In my broken stages I couldn't peace,

Anything together,

Do you really have a choice?

I do,

And I'll never tell you what to do,

Because trying to change someone,

Is difficult as severing a mountain down the middle,

Better yet searching for yourself in a shattered spirit,

Death and time are customized,

Just how character and lifestyle marry each other,

Until what's inside achieves the outcome.

Let Them Hate

Count it as a good thing when haters are cowardice,

To speak and write things to attempt,

To defame your name behind your back,

This is an inclination that you are influencing,

Even the negative with weak character,

You're doing something right,

When an arrogant and gall spirited person,

Dedicates free time to you,

They all think their great actors/actresses,

It is extrinsic motivation,

They should be saying "thank you",

For you making their worldview wider,

And with all that said still can't say it to your face,

Remember when people hate it only makes you great!

~PAIN~

From Understand to Understood

Wisdom might be sorrow,

Knowledge and sacrifice,

The layers of this world are a paradox,

Levels of consciousness in the mind of this battlefield,

Money can get you killed or be a useful tool,

To become who you are there must be proper paths.

The journey of life is uncertain as dirt paths,

Higher level of identity is followed by sorrow,

The streets and corporate places both require tools,

Love versus hate either way we sacrifice,

The faint of fools is a casualty in the battlefield,

Prediction is like wrapping logic around a paradox.

Content with living the experiences in this paradox,

Technology today suggests many paths,

Warriors fight with simplicity in complex battlefields,

Winning doesn't restricts tomorrow's war of sorrow,

Be sure to grin because it's only a sacrifice,

The boon of accepting the truth is a solid tool.

Secrets can be an illusive tool,

Looks are only an image in this paradox,

True self becomes blinded by sacrifice,

If you are not willing to explore there can be no paths,

Not believing in your dream is sorrow,

The ground is cold for snakes to slither the battlefield.

Shattered hearts and broken arrows fill the battlefield,

The tongue is a versatile tool,

Not knowing where one's soul will end up is sorrow,

The past is experience surrounded by a paradox,

Every decision in life has led to these paths,

If I am wrong I can stand behind this sacrifice.

If I am right it will take the ultimate sacrifice,

This earth is an endless battlefield,

Spiritual warfare of good and evil are the main paths,

All players must rely on unspoken rules as a tool,

Welcome to the land of paradox,

Mistakes are a part finding sorrow.

Remains from our sorrows concludes our sacrifice,

The most valuable tool is our mind's battlefield,

Strange enough this paradox guides our paths.

What If I'm wrong?

Could this worldview be an image?

The state of mind a façade,

My plans of the future fraud and only what I want?

Is the opportunity cost moments lost?

The mission to succeed an arrogant reflection of me,

No longer being impulsive has casted people away,

When I was at my worse we would talk all day,

Maybe I got it wrong?

The truth I live by is legitimate in my eyes,

Content with humble pride,

Taking ownership for past defaults,

Keeps dark thoughts in vaults,

Living life as simple as possible,

So, I don't destroy my "self" with complexity,

Where would I be,

If I based my life from what people think about me?

Probably beneath the feet of enemies,

And someone other than me,

Maybe I was always wrong?

Sacrificing time and earthly pleasures for inner peace,

Are worth it now,

Always asking questions to challenge facts of scholars,

Brings me to ask,

What if they are wrong?

Society is innate to its existence,

Whether evaluations are correct or not,

I am right as of now if I died tonight,

Even if I am wrong.

Paradise of the Mind

Do not be fooled by feeling negative or positive,

Because those words are facts letting truth live,

Maybe the end is dark with pain that soothes?

Equate while finding paths as queens and kings,

Deep roots and grape vines beside rivers of logic,

Night and day these dreams wake me up,

Free of pride it's kind but kills,

This earth is meant for graves,

Peace is sweet when strife's served stale,

To whom will learn to reach love?

The heart rhymes along with hymns above,

As clouds subsides in gravity,

It's time to travel beyond pavement,

The present makes this a significant talent,

Mistakes are part of life,

So, leave your mark.

Just Fly

I image myself at a higher altitude,

I shouldn't be the one asking for money,

But saying now that's funny,

Currency is needed to survive,

The conflict issue when some come up lost,

Missing physically and more often mentally,

Living life for the glamour instead of the glory,

Sometimes I feel like this world tried to abort me,

Many will never know,

Not hearing an answer when I pray why,

Still dreaming as a child wishing I can soar the sky,

If only people knew what I go through,

You wish you could fly too.

This War

Royalty and legends,

I hope I don't die before age 27,

Destinations heaven or hell,

I'd rather leave courageous,

Than a snake coward pushing up flowers,

Let my guard down?

My conscience won't let me,

The reflection reveals an enemy,

Damn, you know me so well,

Using those same tricks of the past,

Which has lost its power,

A worthy challenge is prepared,

I've written prayers on my soul,

Such as psalm's and serenity,

Devil doesn't even update his equipment,

When trying to oppress me,

Thinking about thinking leads to thinking,

Understanding that last line will only create illusions,

Surrender everything until blood circulates,

Ruthless as any two oppositions fighting for territory,

Standing in front of myself.

End of the Weak

If you can with-stand pain,

You can face fame,

And the underhanded schemes that go on in this game,

Never tolerated disrespect to the name,

Infatuated with success flowing through my veins,

Knowledge in my lungs,

Take an oath to stay strong until heaven's home,

Trouble has my address,

So, there's no purpose in running,

I refuse to lose to amuse my frenemies,

I'm not a pawn or a bishop,

King's know when to follow the lead,

While you're down they look around,

Kick than say I helped you,

If love is a weakness everyone is vulnerable,

Speaking from the heart aiming for the heart,

Any day during the week,

Service can be terminated,

Disconnected relationships living in memories,

Some may not see,

Only the almighty will survive this end of the weak.

Love & War

What's affection if hate is close with ease?

Against even odds the world is ice,

Beliefs are things we need,

Nights of gloom while sleep take ticks from clocks,

At times the light is dim but radiates,

Good and bad weighed by justice,

Here to draw lines,

The combat is bloody along scars of hope that heals,

Intuitive signs plus warnings,

The end is near my eyes have seen evil,

Carve my heart where pain and warfare stays,

Battling to find my love in war.

Strange World

If I was in prison,

How many people would come see me?

Everyone divided over zero,

Half-hearted greetings,

No meaning of family, sister or brother,

Disclosing information when pain killed comfort,

Met to many know it all's,

Jealousy that awful cologne,

Smirk using body language,

Value privacy like God's secrets,

Tough decisions of a Pharaoh,

Can't hesitate in war,

Commitment is a weapon,

And many miles of insight,

Destiny and Karma,

Marrying one to avoid the other,

At the same time sleeping by her,

Strange world…

Life Learner

If you don't do it I will,

Handing it to God as a default,

Yet an interval of disguised love,

Thinking of the past how I was wrong,

Flashbacks through music,

Learning was the best thing I did,

Now realizing when you say things like,

"I've given it to God to deal with."

True, True,

But never thought that making no decision is a decision,

And when you wait,

God makes a choice,

Which direction the Most High decides,

Always follows with the question why?

You die many times in this lifetime.

~SACRIFICE~

Forethought

Embedded and entice with the sacrifice of life,

Many detailed dreams through epiphanies,

Thanking God she's not with me,

Better yet not with her,

The birth of my unborn makes me concern,

Under pressure like a faithful preacher,

Emotional concepts of the big picture,

While some relationships are temporary,

Is happiness definite?

I seize to believe that notion,

A potent liar's potion,

Actions influence expression from the heart,

Watch the eyes and believe none what you see,

More myths and suspicious things,

They say it's cheaper to keeper,

I never believed especially if you never had her,

So, she didn't have you,

The Lord work hurts,

Only few are chosen and I'm even less than that,

Best way described is unreal to surreal,

Letting the blood bleed on this paper,

Psalms 35 for the haters,

Pedestrians and spectators,

Despite being human,

Realities a paradox; what if heavens locked?

Blurry from the smoke clouds of destruction,

A piece of peace will not complete autonomy,

Without trials and tribulations,

Would you even be humble or thankful?

Followers controlled with sin can't tell the difference,

Right or wrong?

Do it by yourself if you don't want to get caught,

But know that God watches,

Just Forethought.

<u>No Title</u>

From the beginning to the start,

The blood of ink from this pen,

Reflects my heart,

Somewhere either one day my heart was torn apart,

Searched for love yet it only made destiny hard,

Obtaining happiness all the time can be far,

Finding my mind drift into a dimension of thoughts,

No person understands,

Solidarity created this moment,

To transcend how I live,

Hate nothing but if I had to answer the question,

I would say the past,

It's weird how everyone seems satisfied,

While I'm in a battle waiting for a war to ignite,

Running out of ammunition,

Life is a picture you won't see up close,

Maybe if you view the film clear,

For what it is you might not exist,

Knowing that being understood,

Has been dismissed,

This flow is a technique soothing the spirit,

Time is a melting surface,

Uneven ground which under soldiers are found,

With no crown that are only memories,

Who will remember?

God is the rise before the sun rose,

Life long fight since seeing the light,

I'm not supposed to be here,

Always pay respect to the truth,

Still wondering about Genesis,

Sacrifice of life for life,

Succeeding to negotiate with endurance,

Money inquiries anything however my soul is the key,

Needing not to convince anyone,

I've done bad things and comparing them with others,

No longer interest me,

Anticipating dark nights, I may need to slay,

This bloody ink,

These stitches hold my apperception together,

Love can be complicated,

Keeping my eyes on my right hand,

Although I use my left hand to depart jams,

Distant plans are short as sad songs,

Toward the ledge from this edge,

It is purposeless to request out,

Fear no enemies nor believe in false fantasy,

Growing up learning about greed,

Reality is confusing as the mind of a fiend,

Buying new items will refresh a temporary feeling,

Amongst repressing depression,

Decisions make experience,

Psyche of a loin in this cold jungle,

Encoded are future visionary gleams,

In the collective unconscious waking to nonentity,

People can change or influence,

Suffering seems wrong now,

Chances are bullets in chambers of a reliable revolver,

Coasting this voyage roaming the land,

I realize power keeps me a prisoner sometimes,

Knowing you are....

Try Until I Die

Pen and pad is the only therapy I've ever had,

And find it sad adversaries can't catch on,

I was born alone,

I'll die alone,

Right, wrong or in the middle,

Family won't come see you in the hospital,

My purpose created artful deadly riddles,

Confirming real legitimacy,

People get killed and meet death every day,

So, it's irrelevant to change my ways,

I'd rather influence this scenery,

As long as I know my identity,

I forgive but never forget,

Even if there is no love,

I'm prepared to protect respect,

Until the end of my lifetime,

Nothing beats a failure but a try.

Brother

If I am your brother through monetary contribution,

This is extortion,

If I am only your brother through duty,

I am the dimwit for being used,

If I am your brother for the sake of an image,

This picture reflects the shell of a man,

If I am only your brother to be spoken about,

At miscellaneous drinking sessions,

To remedy low self-esteems and false ego,

Why would you think we're brothers?

Then don't call me brother,

Group narcissism means nothing,

We are brothers under God,

I don't worship idols,

To be subconsciously naïve at unawares,

Is the foundation of a fool oblivious to inner peace?

If you are my brother, be my brother.

Poet Slanger

I am a poet slanger,
Not to be confused with drug dealing,
My trials and tribulations pave this concrete jungle.

My metaphors are like morphine-easing pain,
Hovering over these raw lines of addictive material,
I am a poet slanger.

Nor distorted with a rapper,
Although my hooks are sharp as jabs,
My trials and tribulations pave this concrete jungle.

Expression found in thorough bread hustlers,
The G-Code can never be broken,
I am a poet slanger.

Serpents are in the grass sneaking on the gravel,
My words will have you higher than heaven's ceiling,
My trials and tribulations pave this concrete jungle.

This masterpiece is served to the masses,
Loosen up your body, while your thoughts numb,
I am a poet slanger.
My trials and tribulations pave this concrete jungle.

<u>Some Days</u>

Maybe the day I die you will realize,

To stay depressed is destructive,

Giving could be a prize,

What a hero's journey this life,

How affectionately strong love survives?

Uncomfortable intuition with no regards,

Knowledge is covered by truth,

Question everything amidst discernment,

God lives forever,

Reputation still breathes once your soul leaves,

Roles in this movie follow no script,

Awkward world we operate in,

Where our past envies today.

No Evidence

Times are worse than ever,

Since a certain point in my life,

Known odds were against me,

Only love when my momma kisses me,

Feeling no love is American history,

Because they want to restrict me,

Put me asleep mentally,

Wanting the time bomb to go off,

Resulting from bad chemistry,

Trying to be the best I can be,

There are cities and things I desire to see,

Possessing more than one set of keys,

For access to doors of infinite dreams,

Not talking about living wealthy,

More like everything around feels free,

Writing with sincerity,

Turning G's to Z's,

All evidence inclusive.

Whant

What do you want?

Misspelled purpose with telepathic correction,

Just because one stands on top of motivation,

Doesn't mean there's no higher aptitudes,

Asking God everything again...

Whant

Know, No

Make your moves while you're alive,

Coffin of confidence only leads to a pit,

Even if one doesn't know this,

Please notice,

Whant

What do you want?

Consciousness sets the tone,

Listen to the paint,

Staining interpretation in the mind,

Whant

Write to right

Life has episodes everyone is watching,

Without the narcissistic grandiosity,

Relying on the unknown,

Allowing negativity to taint one's thoughts,

Makes one stumble over obstacles,

It's like being dead trying to find one's way home,

In two realms at the same damn time,

While the world gives you hell,

Unless we're all sleep in this tale,

Whant

Life or death?

What do you want?

Opportunity Costs

Our paths are journeys,

Influenced by pain and pleasure,

The only way to open a door is through awareness,

Fear of the unknown can be mysterious,

One destiny to find another,

Being in two places at once is physically impossible,

In order to exist here there's an expense elsewhere,

So, embrace the price of sacrifice,

For this opportunity to spend time.

My Name is Secret

My name is Secret,

Everyone claims to never know me,

I have no preference whether a lie or true,

Death even knows me,

I stalk confidentiality and murder innocence,

Vanity lusts over my looks,

As well as style,

When I'm spoken about it is always quiet,

Sealed with empty loyalty,

I was here in the beginning of time,

And destroyed many minds,

I am believed with reasonable doubt,

Your ancestors protected me,

No one has seen my face nor knows my name,

You have a better chance,

Wrapping your arms around the world twice,

Before you locate me,

I am enemies-enemy,

The more I am kept the faster I move,

I know your whole family,

Many search for me,

I question truth's identity,

You know me,

My name is Secret.

This Lament Place Again

I don't want to die alone,

Like a starving person resisting death from hunger,

If you fall in love,

Hope someone's there to catch you,

And can forgive your past,

Search for your "self",

Not for yourself in another person,

So, when there is nothing your still healthy,

This scenery is hunting at moments,

Every time you love,

A piece of your hearts organ is given out as a sample,

Where spirits linger time and again,

Sometimes physical love is not enough,

Connection is a weapon,

If you don't use it right people get hurt,

Most want to be perfect,

Some to just be married,

I wonder what God thinks about war?

Answers that can only be delivered in light,

Emotions stalk the air,

My needs are worth dying for,

Whenever wrong is ideal,

It is the first symptom of being love sick,

Get well,

While the benevolent dare asks why and what is that?

With shattered glass and broken rearview mirrors,

Don't look back,

If you are chosen than your autonomy will be filled,

Because desire can be lament,

Decisions alter everything in manifestations,

To live, you must learn to die.

Remember How It Feels to be Forgotten

As I lay on the floor waiting for the ceiling to fall,

My body is wore and tore,

I have run out of fuel for my destination,

Not because of my weakness but my failures of true knowledge,

My flawless ways have left me astray,

Some tired days I cannot speak or say anything,

I'm in a category of my own for this throne,

When you rely blindly on your own powers you are a fool!

Power must come from the spirit within,

Many may have it but fewer maintain it,

Troublesome nights before my eyes,

I use to love to fight,

My strength is only the key hole to the door of my soul,

Which is useless if I don't have my minds key,

I forgot my ambition while selfishly unwrapping this present,

Lessons of confessions of the past,

Searching for stepping stones to make it home,

Cut off the head of wrong to renounce a doomed crown,

You can't touch,

Protected by the Most High trying to remember my third eye,

Forgotten… I remember…

~*RELATIONSHIPS*~

I, Do

I, Do, Love you,

I am who I am,

Knowing you has been enlightening,

Hopefully you're the one,

We even love to laugh,

And talk for hours,

Strengthen each other,

Tonight, I will be thinking of you,

Sometimes when we speak,

I feel crazy,

Seeing it as deep Love, Now.

At this moment,

Standing in front of you,

I ask you to never hate and remain true,

Then, my mirror said,

I, Do.

<u>Vice Versa</u>

If I did you the way you did me,

How far in the future could you see?

Do you see me?

I don't see you.

Maybe if we did things different,

We could have grown to become something,

It's me?

But I know it's you,

Now what should I do?

This is the exit,

I can't forget what you put me through,

To hate you is to love me.

<u>Lust You</u>

Run with thieves become a thief,

My heart pulls so many ways,

Love to love,

No one ever admits lust,

Attraction is mental exhaustion,

If you communicate right,

The signs won't be left behind,

People will do what they want,

Abiding by no regulation or rules,

Speaking on love when it isn't love,

In your heavenly presence,

I must say hell yeah,

There are feelings for you,

I lust you.

<u>They</u>

One hundred rumors are not worth investigating once,

You know what they say...

No what did they say?

No one really knows,

Is that a statement, question or cliché?

Who the hell are they?

Is "they" in heaven?

I assume deep thought makes this quest ambiguous,

I guess when you find "they",

Forever and the beginning will be there,

Out of cite and mind,

If not, Reference who?

Them?

A group of anonymous people,

Anyone versus everyone,

Everything by something,

When you find "they",

Tell "them",

I'm looking for the root to the kemetic truth.

Liars

Liar, you ode for the truth!

Everything you have stolen means nothing,

Those unlimited lies have your eyes red,

And when you talk honesty dies,

While your reaction creates a dumb look,

Smile, another façade, an image that fools many,

Take ownership for your words,

Stop then think about false gain,

Even if you were in front of your Maker,

You wouldn't speak to truth,

Lies searching never,

This is what you made,

Life as a liar will end on a true day.

The Honest Lair

I never understood,

How one could be so evil,

Having bad intentions to hunt down others livelihood,

Honestly not for one minute did I believe you,

Or trust your grins including calm voice,

Making sudden time desist,

Acting genuine without soul,

Not a test of punishment more coded passion,

Thirsty for worry, anxiety and dissension,

References of heartache,

Knowledgeable distinctness,

To know the difference.

Love

Kneeled next to the bed,

Right kneed propped up,

Left kneecap touching the earth,

Ear against chest I can hear nothing,

Matter fact you felt cold,

Great soul when I speak,

Even more affluent when wrote,

Saying I care is an understatement,

Wanting an answer with no question marks,

Better yet expressive,

Not false but true genuineness,

If you pay attention there will be change,

I am consciously aware,

Subtracting the foundation of fear,

Toxic relationships are like jewelry,

You're going to lose it eventually,

Just don't exhaust yourself in this search.

The First and Last Letter

It has been a wonder knowing you,

I hope that you are woman enough to finish this through,

If you happen to delete it I feel like it will still find you,

Interesting to know that we never knew each other but sexually,

You never knew how poetry is in my identity,

And really hated to see your reflection at times,

This is not about rhythm and riddle but made in this form,

To keep your attention,

I've always thought you were caught up in your pretty girl image,

I would cringe because at moments I felt like I would get a call,

That you committed suicide,

Praying for you is what I would and still do,

I hear you and your right I am not perfect but my heart is alive,

Is God a murderer or is that the Goddess in you doing the killing?

Deep I know you must be grown to take this on,

To keep me attached in your life,

When I have nothing to do with your demons,

That visits you every night,

It is only right I ask with no expectations,

This is not judging if it is a true fact,

I don't know what my pride has to do with this?

This is not a plea but a sensible creed,

Because if it wasn't I couldn't finish this letter,

Marriage is not a career and it seems like your scared to be alone,

This is not a dig at you if time aligns,

We are missing the volume in this song and that is a pun,

These words may seem vicious but this is true letter poetry,

And knowing you then you had a great heart!

I know that you will act like you never read this,

Which is cool to flow with the current,

If I died you will know how it feels to not have me exist,

You can continue to mourn secretly,

The same reason you say the past is not important,

None of this is written out of spite or illegitimate respect,

So, you believe beauty is your curse?

Just don't believe in it and it will go away,

This is the only poem I've written to fit your skin,

Try it on with no fear,

Which is why you can fall in love simply by choosing,

When I seen that wicked smile when you drove off I knew,

You love no one but you,

But when you whispered about us no one knew,

That's alright with me because that's not my life,

One day we will realize we're not friends,

And before you count this a love letter re-read it,

You're a desperate lover cheating with ideals,

Be sure not to let this stroke your ego,

Stepping outside myself I can see how this is entertaining,

Have ever tried to save someone from drowning?

You would understand,

I am a true man that can express my soul through a pen,

Plus, I know how to write even when I'm not right,

Many of these lines to an outsider would be misunderstood,

Unless you gave them a real look into your eyes,

My last advice is don't be wicked,

Don't allow this world to ruin your true spirit or mindset of others,

Although I've been gone and can't come back,

First and Last...

Peace

Jealous of Love

Why do you love to hate me?

I am not scared to take a risk for you,

But, how you treat me is like low hanging fruit,

Too much in common has numb my tolerance,

You're personality conflicts with mine,

No essence to the element,

Jealous of Love...

So cold, So expressive, So what?

Favor is far more better than luck,

Love teaches me,

Reaches me with no pleas,

While the past needs me,

Jealous of love... How?

This internal strife knew this wife,

Love is God so are you jealous of the Most High?

That divine energy was never in the sky,

Or mind it lies in the soul,

Jealous of Love?

Naw, because my heart is full of love,

And if I was jealous I wouldn't know you, Love...

~POETIC VAULT~

<u>Worry</u>

I worry about my heart because I don't trust you,

Remember the day I said "I Love you",

How I know your committed is when you say "I Hate you"

I'm an introvert with extroverted ways,

So, marry perception if you want to,

Living in the future will make your past hunt you,

I'm worried if I think higher if it would make me too new,

But knew misery was ahead,

Damn, that sounds crazy when I say it,

I worry about how nobody knows me,

If it wasn't for my two seeds I couldn't have grown me,

My current presence depicts a different definition of a "G",

I see many bad things but I won't talk,

It's funny how everyone says they know God?

Think about it while I pause,

I'm worried because that just threw you off,

Let me get humorous so you don't think I'm losing it,

Laughing at my enemies,

They shot and missed,

I threw back clips so they can see,

Pretending to be happy with that social media personality,

I'm worried for the fact that face-to-face talk is ol' skool,

Life experience will always make you a new fool,

I'm no longer worried,

I was just like you,

Worry made me paranoid and then fall in love with the truth,

Live now and don't worry about death,

Because what you hear at this moment is what's left.

Don't' worry because soon you will forget...

Worry

Challenge...

Ran away to only fall into a safety net called comfort,

Like a grave being dug for rest,

It was a mindful exchange and was everlasting,

I'm sure in a past lifetime our spirits were together,

Write as we are trying to right our biggest howevers,

Amazed that you see my complexity,

Very certain you can see you in me,

And our ways are similar in attracting energy,

I know that you have been patient with me and you can see,

It wasn't difficult to hear the universe heart throb,

And when you showed up we knew,

I will admit that I have been self-conscious about vulnerability,

There is this potent antidote to be high on lust,

If I was to be addicted to anything I rather be on love,

Your clever ability to see past my distractions keeps me,

Is it possible to be friends with an ex-enemy?

If forgiven how come you don't understand the principle of love?

And the answer you gave elaborate on experience and errors,

I don't believe that some ex-lovers can ever be healed,
That door is shut forever,
The cliché goes "Never say never but there are some Nevers"

I feel like I can fall in love again after all my mistakes,
Her soul is rich with expression embedded with support,
I'm learning not to regret so I look past her,

At times I can come off absent-minded and cold but I am loving,
My intuition tells me that she can care for my spirit,
I desire to show you, who I am because we are so similar,

Hearts gravitate towards one another due to mirrored strife,
If I've had such a broken heart than what does that say about you?
The way we mental stimulate each other provides me hope,

I am thankful for her grace because I remember,
"If you knew how exclusive I am you would understand,"
This challenge is worth fighting for and I will not run away,

I want to learn more about her vulnerable true self,

Understanding is the best way to give another person a piece,

I am anxious to transcend to the next stage of peace,

Which I can't do alone.

Acoustic Heart Strings

This feeling other than a reason,

Real bold crimson color lipstick,

Without words your mouth said kiss,

Presence like gold let them keep the dimes,

So gorgeous can give a blind man sight,

Know you ain't right and that body tight,

Deep listener probably loves to cook,

Yehwah just blessed me,

Owedishalew,

I hear your loud soul,

Love's instrument,

Music to my heart I can take a dart,

Smile can illuminate the dark,

It's not my fault my heart was in a vault,

My queen, king do anything,

Even slay a loin,

I'm not lyin',

I want to keep you happy,

82

Crack up laughing over this compassionate challenge,

Insane attraction I know what happen,

Healthy sense of humor,

Can't take you serious half the time,

Not particular but picky tho,

I think you get me yo,

I'm in full pursuit and I will take a clue,

You're not the only one that's impatient,

My mind gone plus my covers blown,

What you wanna do?

You say I don't have sense but you're a Goddess sent,

I'd hold you like a guitar,

There is a God...

Only One

I am honored to receive a poem from you,

It's evident that my absent mindlessness showed,

You're so understanding until there is disrespect,

Because you're a real woman,

So, it's not all about sex or a check,

Whenever I read your poems,

You give it your best,

And when I am distracted by life,

You may feel neglect which would hurt me,

An eye for an eye would make us both not see,

You're so loving and patient to the point,

I feel I need you around me to balance my thoughts,

It is scary in a good way,

No holding back on my end,

I want to be your compassionate friend than more,

I never met to offend you,

And my presences desires to be near you,

I've thought if you could be the one as well,

Because there are no awkward moments,

And when we use to sit at the restaurants,

I felt like you were my therapist,

Need to resolve my mind,

I could be away from you for a long time,

But whenever you respond it's like we never left.

Exit Strategy

She doesn't want to hear about her opinion,

And come to a crossroad to stay or go,

About me...

This hesitation is more apprehension to not be in a relationship,

No trauma, drama nor a woman named Karma,

Made this influenced way,

As a young man I was brave,

And as a grown man I know the difference,

Because I have always been ahead of my time,

Forcing me to choose protection over comfort,

Not to be unhappy but to never lose my "self",

Which usually doesn't impute with the risk,

The truth is that is gets difficult to only focus on this,

Because I am selfish and trying to be more warming,

There is a hesitation in my cooperation to learn patience,

Being too honest can push people into categories,

And often indirectly becoming another page in my story,

She thinks I procrastinate but I feel I'm taken my time,

In her eyes the expectations are just as important as fantasy,

And if it is only one person in it she would say,

Well you don't need me...

Hidden behind something implies that one is intimidated,

I am stand in front of myself,

Leaving the past at the curb of wasted opportunity,

My mind wants to explore more,

While the heart needs warmth in this cold storm,

Maybe trust and secure love is too far?

My ambition won't allow me to give up,

Just as one cannot make someone care who doesn't care,

You can't make someone be there that doesn't want to be there,

Typically, when a person has demands this means,

Either they are saving you and/or saving you from them...

I know this is an intricate view to truly show me.

At the same moment not hiding anything...

No Restriction

Her mind is focused when asking questions,
When she is challenged it seems as,
If there is a relief to be mentally exhausted,

Intuitive beyond the norm and aware,
Knowing that one's thought are engraved into the spirit,
Not heard like old voicemail messages,

To deny true-identity would be to prohibit love,
Paying attention to every choice of word,
And how long it takes to respond back,

Modest with a way of getting that point precise,
Forgiving if done right than don't apologize at all,
To cross that line will be a treacherous fall,

This loyalist is not confused when rules are broken,
And even though she loves spoken words of affirmation,
Her stare makes statements,

Serious answers become a compliment to uncomfortable,
So, when that day comes one can "know this" instead of notice,
Her tongue is sharp but gentle,

And can discard an ex-loved,
With the slay of the pencil in a journal,
Why not use a pen?

Or a permanent maker?
Because when you use a pencil,
You can always start all over again…

Tell Me...

Her inquisitive nature to be deliberate,

This irony runs over my thoughts at times,

Because to divulge may require all her talents as a helper,

It could be too much to handle let alone tolerate,

I've lied and survived wicked people that live in evil,

This pain is hard to explain with words even if I could trust,

Never allowing myself to be loved is true,

And my flaws are deeper than the Nile river flow,

When you ask me questions you challenge me to think about you,

I want to teach her so many things with my lips,

Knowledge from a kiss is what keeps me wanting more,

Her analytical mind keeps me thinking about thinking,

She mentions spiritual, sexual and intent,

Which are three things to be honest I cannot resist,

The bedroom with her would transform into a pleasure abyss,

Since I responded with ask me anything,

Hopefully now you can tell me everything,

And don't worry it won't scare me,

Leading to these questions for her,

If you have never been in love,

Than how do you know what love is?

Can you take it without giving it?

How do I know you are telling me the truth?

Ask Me Anything

This first impression has led to a road of thought,

You have woken me,

She is sure of her "self" when she challenges others,

Because it seems like she loves to love,

And has this dedication to be a loyal romantic,

I could be wrong but when we dialogue,

It's like two artists writing a hit song,

Her opinion alone had me starring,

I can tell she has cried over time,

And it's been a long time since I've seen such honest eyes,

I despise lies and know because I had to clear my vision,

Which means she knows what she wants,

Even if I were to front,

She would still want to learn something,

It's more than physical because when the mind is intimate,

We become an "individual",

Her energy radiates so passionately,

She makes Denver winters feel like Harlem summer heat,

With her careful body language and intense looks,

While I watch her put on her favorite lip-gloss seductively,

When she goes for what she wants she has this walk,

Keeping me intrigued to listen when she wants to talk,

Time went faster than quick sand but was calm as a river bank,

We both have defense mechanisms to justify detachment,

In this chance interaction I was asked a question about love,

That affirmed I was previously in lust,

Until now this set me further free from that old rigid me,

So, when I give her more she can ask me anything.

Dear Hennessy

Far beyond thought to find my bounds,

Pouring liquor for my loved one's underground,

The sacrifice to unlearn depends on the pain to bring closure,

Repeating this sip like a skipped CD,

It seems as if everyone thinks they know the truth,

Honest lips for a drunk mind makes for nights like this,

The soul yearns for this spirit that hides behind these eyes,

Living in my mind like it is a concentration camp,

Trying to walk this line knowing I'm not making it home,

I landed on the wrong planet,

So, I cheer to war,

Only time I drink like this is when I'm hurt to the core,

Taking the blame for my position in life channels strife,

Life is a bitch so it's a canine's world,

Monies a dictator of control and bloodshed,

White supremacy aims to dim enlightenment,

Ignorance is not the new black,

I'm not rambling because it's the truth Jack,

But prefer cognac,

When its war time I won't need a mask,

Words speak to my soul like Jazz,

Stomach touching my back,

Filling up my glass,

Access in knowledge,

This can only grow from what you know,

No, it's not just about being present,

Wisdom serving as a weapon,

If this is my last poetry entry,

And you drink nothing from this cup,

Remember not to jeopardize your soul for this spirit,

Because I only make you feel good,

When you are my addiction.

Miss, You

Walking into this space I feel misplaced,

Recipe for a grandiose mistake,

Broken trust made me want to dodge misconception,

I can't interrupt miscommunications,

Fake boss talk is miscellaneous,

That stare don't make me scared you misunderstood,

At least I get it so fitted but you missed,

Don't leave voicemails over misconduct,

If I was a book I'd be misread,

I can help but won't be misused,

This moral compasses has a misdirection,

Lived in the past tense with shoulders storing my mishaps,

Too many thoughts are on trial I'm misjudged,

Enlightened spirit I find you in misbelief...

<u>Colorism</u>

Drowned Love,

Abused Healing,

Raped Freedom,

And Murdered the collective truth…

Wisdom Is Sorrow

Looking in the eyes of this homeless man that lives in a mansion,

Monies something but it means nothing when your bleeding,

Close your mouth lets speak,

I'm here to hear everything,

Need a tune-up on my Chakras,

Protect my crown like an undefeated mobster,

Where is a place every human will be in their time?

It's a "grave" concept,

Which is why when people that are dying want to live,

Could be an assumption from my spiritual function,

Your past is a shadow when you live in the light,

No insurance but I made it out the fast life,

Especially when you know you ain't right,

Lying saying you alright,

It's a cruel world and perception of man in power are evil,

Because you know what's going to happen….

Other Books by Black Ausar:

Philosophical Poetry: Crowns & Shattered Dreams

Sufferless: Meditations for Transforming Trauma into Healing

From the book:

Philosophical Poetry: Crowns & Shattered Dreams

Rest in Peace Old Me

Let them envy,
If anything that's gasoline,
To my destination,
Tall influence,
So, I don't get short changed,
Wasn't always who I am now,
Cold as no love,
Transitioned into a Healer,
My road led to becoming an Empath,
Weak jaws would get stiff jabs,
Can't miss what I never had,
Unforgiveness was my norm,
A young man that loved anger,
Replaced rage with sage,
Life happens in intervals,
To be who I am today,
Was ordained,
Not a miracle,
Brush this dirt off me,
I died to myself,
I'm born again,
Rise. New. Me.

-Black Ausar

HOTEP

Made in the USA
Middletown, DE
31 August 2024

60077757R00061